www.thefoodteacher.co.uk

Acknowledgements

The assistance of all the pilot schools in supporting the development of these materials is gratefully acknowledged.

Specific thanks to Manland Primary School, Attleborough Infant School, Harpenden Academy and Larwood School for their support and detailed feedback.

Special thanks to Katy Wilmshurst, Penny Bird and Camera, Luke Godward (design) and Sue Tate.

Above all an extra special thanks to Tim and Alice for all your help, support and taste testing.

Disclaimer

The author wishes to make it clear that they accept no responsibility for any liability, loss or risk, personal or otherwise, which is incurred as a result of using any of the recipes and/or recommendations suggested herein. It is the users responsibility to ensure that any information or ingredients are suitable for those who will consume them. If in any doubt, or if requiring medical advice, please contact the appropriate health professional.

All rights reserved. No part of this publication may be reproduced, stored in a retrieval system, or transmitted in any form or by any means, electronic, mechanical, photocopying, recording or otherwise, without prior written consent of the author.

First published in Great Britain by Katharine Tate, The Food Teacher in 2015.

Contents

4	Introduction	46	Key Stage 2 Recipes
6	Overview of Cooking and Nutrition Curriculum	48	Guacamole
8	National Curriculum and Progression	50	Coleslaw
10	Key Cookery Skills	52	Couscous Salad
13	Equipment Checklist	56	Chunky Hummus
14	Key Stage 1 Recipes	58	Egg Mayonnaise Spiders
16	Tomato and Prawn Lettuce Wraps	60	Pitta Pockets
18	Tuna Dip	64	Greek Salad
20	Smashed Bean Dip	66	Sour Cream and Chive Dip
24	Mackerel Pâté	68	Paprika Dip
26	Three Bean Salad	72	Spiral Sandwiches/Wraps
28	Veggie Kebabs	74	Layered Rainbow Salad
32	Jewelled Rice/Pasta Salad	76	Make Your Own Muesli
34	Finger Sandwiches	80	Avocado and Lime Mousse
36	Fruit Kebabs	82	Green Smoothie
40	Avocado Orange Chocolate Mousse	84	Apricot Seed Bars
42	Pineapple Smoothie	86	Nutrition Know How
44	Raspberry Punch	90	Glossary
		92	How the Food Teacher Can Help You

Introduction

This book is the first of a series that illustrates how an aspect of the Cooking and Nutrition National Curriculum for Key Stage 1 and 2 can be delivered in classrooms.

This book, 'No Kitchen Cookery' aims to give teachers an outline for cookery lessons with objectives, outcomes and assessment opportunities identified. Greater emphasis is placed on savoury dishes as suggested within the National Curriculum.

Recipes are mapped to the curriculum showing progression alongside key cookery skills that children can experience and demonstrate as they create the recipes. The recipes are aimed to appeal to children, are purposeful (e.g. snack, lunch), accessible to all and fun.

The pages are colour coded with green containing information needed by teachers and purple for the pupil recipe pages.

It is suggested all lessons are 1 hour long and opportunities to talk about what sort of food the children are cooking with and where the food comes from should be built into the learning. Dietary adaptations have been suggested where appropriate, which can also provide an additional area for discussion in the classroom.

It is also important for the teacher to model food safety and discuss concepts like washing hands, washing foods before preparation and keeping food covered and in fridges.

All recipes serve between 4-12, so quantities of ingredients need to be calculated for whole class sessions.

Schools organise classroom cookery sessions in many different ways. Some practices I have experienced include:
- Parents being given the recipe a week before and children bringing all the necessary ingredients into school. If you choose to do this it is recommended parents ask children to weigh and measure ingredients themselves at home so that learning opportunities are not missed.
- Teacher/support assistant or catering staff buy ingredients for the class. Some schools ask parents for a half-termly/termly contribution.

This book contains all that is needed to deliver cookery without a kitchen in your school.

Forthcoming books include 'Classroom Baking' and 'Flip Learning Cookery', which encompass other aspects of the Cooking and Nutrition National Curriculum for Key Stage 1 and 2.

About the Author

The Food Teacher, Katharine Tate, has worked as a teacher and education consultant internationally in primary and secondary schools for over 20 years. Qualified as a registered nutritional therapist, Katharine combines her unique education and nutrition expertise to offer schools, organisations and families advice, education programmes, practical workshops, and individual/family consultations.

Katharine Tate, The Food Teacher
BEd (Hons), FAETC, Dip ION (Distinction), BANT, CNHC

© The Food Teacher

Overview of Cooking and Nutrition Curriculum
Key Stage 1 & 2

The content of the 'cooking and nutrition' programmes of study indicate knowledge, skills and understanding that underpin high quality designing and making with food. Pupils should only be taught the parts of 'designing and making' that are relevant to food. When working with food, use a range of domestic, local and industrial contexts appropriate to pupils' ages, for example health, home, garden, leisure, culture, food industry and agriculture.

Main themes:

1 Healthy eating and nutrition
The emphasis here is on application, not just knowledge. Consider the building blocks – from knowing about different foods, at least 5-a-day, recommended eating plate and tips for healthy eating through to energy, nutrients, dietary needs and health. Look at recipes and menus and discuss what could be changed, how ingredients could be prepared differently for health and reading food labels to make smart choices. Aspects can also be covered in practical lessons, helping to apply theory in a meaningful way.

2 Cooking — Focus on the skills
Ensure that a range of skills are covered. Look at a range of techniques, using different ingredients. Ask children and young people what they like to cook – you may be surprised. In primary school, cooking activities can and should happen – get yourself confident with non-cook dishes to start. While food safety and hygiene isn't mentioned, it still needs to be taught.

3 Where food comes from
Make the link back to the principles that our food and drink has to be grown, reared, caught and processed – it really doesn't just appear by magic! Grow your own food – it could just be tomatoes or potatoes in a bucket. Investigate recipes and use maps to work out where food comes from. Ask questions –how is a cow milked? And if you can, go on a farm visit – a memorable experience for life.

'Cooking and nutrition' should be taught as part of 'designing and making'.

© The Food Teacher

National Curriculum and Progression
Key Stage 1
(NC Document, Design and Technology Association)

Checklist

Pupils should be taught to...		Pupils should know...	Pages
...use the basic principles of a healthy and varied diet to prepare dishes	• Basic principles – e.g. name and sort foods into food groups. • Taught that a healthy diet contains a balance of the food groups and should contain a rainbow of fruit and vegetables daily. • Prepare dishes – make a range of simple dishes without a heat source e.g. dips, salads, sandwiches and fruit kebabs/salads.	• How to name and sort foods into different food groups • That everyone should eat at least five portions of fruit and veg. daily • How to prepare simple dishes safely and hygienically, without using a heat source • How to use techniques such as cutting, peeling and grating	16, 18, 20, 24, 26, 28, 32, 34, 36, 40, 42, 44
... understand where food comes from	• Understand where food comes from - should know that all food comes from plants or animals and that food has to be farmed, grown elsewhere or caught.	• That all food comes from plants or animals • That food has to be farmed, grown elsewhere	16, 18, 20, 24, 26, 28, 34, 40

(Source: Adapted from NC Document, Design and Technology Association)

National Curriculum and Progression
Key Stage 2

(NC Document, Design and Technology Association)

Checklist

Pupils should be taught to...		Pupils should know...	Pages
...understand and apply the principles of a healthy and varied diet	• Principles of a healthy and varied diet – understand that a healthy diet is made up from a variety and balance of different foods and drinks. To be active and healthy, food is needed to provide energy for the body. A variety of food is needed in the diet because different foods contain different nutrients that are needed for health	• That a healthy diet is made up from a variety and balance of different food and drinks • That to be active and healthy, food and drink are needed to provide energy for the body • That different food and drink contain different substances – nutrients, water and fibre – that are needed for health	48, 50, 52, 56, 58, 60, 64, 66, 68, 72, 74, 76, 80, 82, 84
...prepare and cook a variety of predominantly savoury dishes using a range of cooking techniques	• Prepare and cook – pupils should create, plan, prepare and cook a range of food dishes, including those which require the use of heat sources • Predominantly savoury dishes – using a range of food groups • Range of cooking techniques – experience of a variety of techniques, e.g. learn how to peel, chop, slice, grate, mix, spread, knead and bake	• How to use a range of techniques such as peeling, chopping, slicing, grating, mixing, spreading, kneading and baking • How to prepare and cook a variety of predominantly savoury dishes safely and hygienically including, where appropriate, the use of a heat source • That recipes can be adapted to change the appearance, taste, texture and aroma	48, 50, 52, 56, 58, 60, 64, 66, 68, 72, 74, 76, 80, 82, 84

© The Food Teacher

Pupils should be taught to...		Pupils should know...	Pages
...understand seasonality, and know where and how a variety of ingredients are grown, reared, caught and processed	• Understand seasonality – which can affect food availability • Grown, reared, caught – know that food is grown (such as tomatoes, wheat and potatoes), reared (such as pigs, chickens and cattle) and caught (such as fish) in the UK, Europe and the wider world • Processed – food produced is processed into ingredients that can be eaten or used in cooking, for example grain is milled to produce flour, oil is pressed from olives, butter is made from milk	• That food is grown (such as tomatoes, wheat and potatoes), reared (such as pigs, chickens and cattle) and caught (such as fish) in the UK, Europe and the wider world • That seasons may affect the food available • How food is processed into ingredients that can be eaten or used in cooking	56, 58, 74

(Source: Adapted from NC Document, Design and Technology Association)

Key Cookery Skills

(Adapted from Cooking in School, Focus on Food, Food for Life Partnership)

Knife Skills

Skill	Ingredients for skill practice	Recipe numbers	R	Y1	Y2	Y3	Y4	Y5	Y6
Cutting food with scissors	Apricots, dates	32, 52, 74, 76, 84	●	●	●	●	●	●	●
Bridge knife techniques — soft foods	Strawberry, cherry tomato	16, 34, 36, 40, 42, 44, 58, 60, 72, 74, 76, 80, 84	●	●	●	●	●	●	●
Bridge knife technique — harder foods	Apple	50, 60, 72, 74			●	●	●	●	●
Claw knife technique — soft foods	Cucumber	28, 60, 66, 68, 72, 74, 76		●	●	●	●	●	●
Claw knife technique — harder foods	Carrot	60, 66, 72, 74				●	●	●	●
Simple combination of bridge and claw	Onion, orange	48, 50, 52, 64, 74, 82						●	●
Fine chopping of herbs	Chives, parsley, coriander	48							●
Snipping herbs in a jug using scissors	Chives, parsley, coriander	24, 32, 48, 66		●	●	●	●	●	●
Peeling soft vegetables	Courgette						●	●	●
Peeling harder vegetables	Carrot, potato	50						●	●
Grating soft foods	Courgette, cheese	40, 60, 80, 84				●	●	●	●
Grating harder foods	Carrot, apple	50, 60					●	●	●

© The Food Teacher

Skill	Ingredients for skill practice	Recipe numbers	R	Y1	Y2	Y3	Y4	Y5	Y6
Finer grating	Parmesan cheese, nutmeg	80					●	●	●

Weighing and Measuring

Skill	Ingredients for skill practice	Recipe numbers	R	Y1	Y2	Y3	Y4	Y5	Y6
Using measuring spoons and cups	Spices, herbs, oil	16, 18, 20, 24, 26, 32, 40, 42, 50, 52, 56, 58, 64, 66, 68, 74, 76, 82	●	●	●	●	●	●	●
Using a jug to measure liquids	Juice, oil, milk	42, 44, 66, 82			●	●	●	●	●
Using balance scales	Beans, fish, yoghurt	32, 52, 64, 68	●	●	●	●	●	●	●
Counting out ingredients	Fruits, vegetables	28, 36, 64	●	●	●	●	●	●	●
Using digital or spring balance scales	Beans, fish, yoghurt	32, 52, 64, 68				●	●	●	●

Other

Skill	Ingredients for skill practice	Recipe numbers	R	Y1	Y2	Y3	Y4	Y5	Y6
Tearing	Herbs	24, 32	●	●	●	●	●	●	●
Crumbling cheese	Feta cheese	18, 24, 52	●	●	●	●	●	●	●
Arranging ingredients/toppings	Layered salad	60	●	●	●	●	●	●	●
Spreading with the back of a spoon	Pizza topping	34, 72	●	●	●	●	●	●	●
Spreading with a table knife	Butter	34, 72			●	●	●	●	●
Scooping	Jacket potato		●	●	●	●	●	●	●

© The Food Teacher

Skill	Ingredients for skill practice	Recipe numbers	R	Y 1	Y 2	Y 3	Y 4	Y 5	Y 6
Mashing	Beans, potato, avocado	20, 40, 42, 44, 48, 56, 80		•	•	•	•	•	•
Crushing garlic	Garlic	48, 56, 68			•	•	•	•	•
Using a lemon squeezer	Lemon, lime, orange	16, 18, 20, 24, 40, 42, 44, 48, 52, 64, 66, 80	•	•	•	•	•	•	•
Mixing/beating ingredients together	Salad dressing, scrambled eggs	16, 18, 20, 24, 26, 32, 40, 44, 48, 50, 56, 58, 64, 66, 68, 76, 80, 84	•	•	•	•	•	•	•
Using a blender	Smoothie	82, 84					•	•	•
Whisking	Smoothies, egg whites, cream	26, 42				•	•	•	•
Shelling a hard boiled egg	Egg	58, 74				•	•	•	•
Garnishing and decorating	Herbs, paprika, cinnamon	16, 18, 20, 34, 40, 52, 58, 74	•	•	•	•	•	•	•
Seasoning to taste	Salt and pepper	48					•	•	•
Using a toaster	Bread	60					•	•	•
Using a rolling pin	Pastry, bread	72	•	•	•	•	•	•	•
Washing/draining through a sieve or colander	Lettuce, beans, vegetables	16, 20, 26, 28, 32, 34, 36, 44, 50, 56, 60, 64, 66, 68, 72, 74, 76, 82		•	•	•	•	•	•

Baking skills (not included in these recipes)

1. Sieving e.g. flour
2. Cutting fat into flour
3. Cracking an egg
4. Separating an egg
5. Beating an egg
6. Rubbing fat into flour
7. Adding liquid to flour
8. All-in-one cake mixing
9. Creaming fat and sugar
10. Folding flour into creamed mixture
11. Scraping out a bowl with spatula
12. Dividing mixture into tins e.g. muffins
13. Mixing to form a bread dough
14. Kneading
15. Shaping e.g. bread rolls
16. Handling and folding filo pastry
17. Handling and rolling puff pastry
18. Handling and rolling short crust pastry
19. Cutting out rolled pastry
20. Glazing e.g. brushing with egg, milk, oil

© The Food Teacher

Equipment Checklist

(This is a comprehensive equipment checklist for the curriculum. Please note that the equipment in italics is not required for the recipes in this book)

Knife skills

- ☐ Chopping board
- ☐ Vegetable knife
- ☐ Kitchen scissors
- ☐ Grater
- ☐ Peeler

Weighing and measuring

- ☐ Measuring spoons, cups
- ☐ Measuring Jug
- ☐ Weighing Scales

Baking skills

- ☐ Rolling pin
- ☐ Baking trays/tins
- ☐ Blender
- ☐ Toaster
- ☐ *Oven/hob/microwave*
- ☐ *Brush (glazing)*
- ☐ *Saucepans*
- ☐ *Wire cooling racks*
- ☐ *Food processor*

Other skills

- ☐ Table knife, fork, spoon
- ☐ Mixing bowl
- ☐ Potato masher
- ☐ Can opener
- ☐ Garlic press
- ☐ Kettle
- ☐ Glasses, plates, bowls (serving)
- ☐ Sieve/ Colander
- ☐ Whisk
- ☐ Lemon juicer
- ☐ Ladle
- ☐ Wooden spoon
- ☐ Spatula
- ☐ Cutters (biscuits, scones)

© The Food Teacher

Key Stage 1
Recipes

Tomato and Prawn Lettuce Wraps
Serves 6-8

Learning Objectives

- Create a simple dish using a recipe
- Awareness that different foods offer different nutrients
- Understand where prawns and vegetables come from (animal/plant)

Learning Outcomes

- Bridge knife technique, measuring and using a squeezer
- Prepared dish
- Can explain where prawns and vegetables come from (animal/plant)

Aim

Children to create a simple savoury dish

Assessment

- Skills
- Understanding of difference between animal and plant

Skills Checklist

Knife Skills	Weighing and Measuring	Baking	Other
• Bridge knife technique	• Using measuring spoons • Using balance scales		• Washing and draining through a colander/sieve • Beating ingredients together (dressing) • Using a lemon squeezer • Garnishing

© The Food Teacher

Dietary Adaptations

Dairy free – soya yoghurt/mayonnaise

Tomato and Prawn Lettuce Wraps
Serves 6-8

Equipment

Teaspoon
Tablespoon
Mixing spoon
Mixing bowl
Colander/sieve
Lemon juicer
Plate for serving
Kitchen paper
Weighing scales

Ingredients

2 little gem lettuces
220g (8oz.) cooked peeled prawns

For the dressing:
½ lemon or lime
3 tbsp. natural Greek yoghurt
2 tsp. tomato purée
½ tsp. paprika

Method

1. Separate the lettuce leaves and put into your colander/sieve.
2. Wash in cold water.
3. Pat dry with the kitchen paper and lay out on the serving plate.
4. Now wash your prawns in the colander and pat dry.
5. Lay 3 or 4 prawns on each lettuce leaf.

Make the dressing

1. Squeeze the lemon or lime into the mixing bowl.
2. Add the yoghurt and tomato purée.
3. Stir together until you have a pink dressing.
4. Add 2 tsps. of dressing to each lettuce leaf.
5. Sprinkle the paprika on top to finish.

Nutrition know how

- Prawns live in the sea and they are high in protein, which helps our bodies to build and repair.

- Tomato purée contains vitamin C, which is good for our teeth and gums and helps us to absorb iron from our food.

Tuna Dip
Serves 6-8

Learning Objectives

- Create a simple dip using a recipe
- Measure quantities using teaspoons and tbsp.
- Understand why fish is important for our brains

Aim

Children to create a simple dip

Assessment

- Skills
- Some awareness of the nutritional value of fish

Learning Outcomes

- Use of measuring spoons, lemon squeezer
- Prepared dish
- Can explain what fish contains for brain health

Skills Checklist

Knife Skills	Weighing and Measuring	Baking	Other
	• Using measuring spoons		• Flaking food (tuna) • Mixing ingredients together • Using a lemon squeezer • Garnishing

© The Food Teacher

Dietary Adaptations

Dairy free – soya yoghurt/mayonnaise

Tuna Dip
Serves 6-8

Equipment

Teaspoon
Tablespoon
Mixing spoon
Mixing bowl
Colander/sieve
Lemon juicer
Plate for serving
Kitchen paper

Ingredients

1 tin (160g) tuna

For the dressing:
½ lemon
3 tbsp. natural Greek yoghurt
½ tsp. mustard
½ tsp. paprika
Decoration - chives

Method

1. Open the tin of tuna and drain away any liquid.
2. Put the tuna into a mixing bowl and use the fork to break it into flakes.

Make the dressing
1. Squeeze the lemon into the mixing bowl with the tuna.
2. Add the yoghurt and mustard.
3. Mix well.
4. Spoon into the serving bowl and sprinkle the paprika on top to finish.
5. Decorate with chives

(For serving – you could include oat cakes, carrot or celery)

Nutrition know how

Tuna is an oily fish, which is high in omega-3 fatty acids. These are important for our brain to work and grow as these fats provide us with lots of energy.
Omega-3 fatty acids may help our brain with learning and memory.

© The Food Teacher

Smashed Bean Dip
Serves 6-8

Learning Objectives

- Create a simple dip using a recipe
- Measure quantities using teaspoons and tbsp.
- Understand why legumes can benefit our health

Learning Outcomes

- Use of measuring spoons, lemon squeezer, masher
- Prepared dish
- Can explain why legumes benefit our health

Aim

Children to create a simple dip

Assessment

- Skills
- Some awareness of the nutritional value of legumes

Skills Checklist

Knife Skills	Weighing and Measuring	Baking	Other
	• Using measuring spoons		• Washing and draining through a sieve/colander • Mashing • Beating ingredients together (dressing) • Using a lemon squeezer • Garnishing

Dietary Adaptations

Dairy free – soya yoghurt/mayonnaise

Smashed Bean Dip
Serves 6-8

Equipment

Teaspoon
Tablespoon
Mixing spoon
Fork
Potato masher
Mixing bowl
Colander/sieve
Lemon juicer
Bowl for serving

Ingredients

1 tin (400g) cannellini beans
1 tin (400g) chickpeas

For the dressing:
½ lemon
4 tbsp. natural Greek yoghurt
2 tsp. cumin
1 tsp. olive oil
1 tsp. mixed seeds

Method

1. Open the tin of beans and chickpeas.
2. Put into colander/sieve and rinse under water and drain.
3. Pour into the mixing bowl and crush with a fork and/or masher.

Make the dressing
1. Squeeze the lemon into the mixing bowl with the beans and peas.
2. Add the yoghurt, oil and cumin.
3. Mix well.
4. Spoon into the serving bowl and sprinkle the mixed seeds on top to finish.

(For serving – you could include rice crackers, carrot or celery)

Nutrition know how

Chickpeas and cannellini beans are both known as legumes and grow from plants. They contain a lot of protein, minerals and fibre, which help our digestion and can keep our energy and concentration levels even throughout the day.

© The Food Teacher

Mackerel Pâté
Serves 4

Learning Objectives

- Create a simple pâté following a recipe
- Cut herbs in a jug using scissors
- Understand why fish is important for our brains

Learning Outcomes

- Use of measuring spoons, lemon squeezer, scissors
- Prepared dish
- Can explain what fish contains for brain health

Aim

Children to create a fish pâté

Assessment

- Skills
- Some awareness of the nutritional value of fish

Skills Checklist

Knife Skills	Weighing and Measuring	Baking	Other
• Cutting herbs using scissors	• Using measuring spoons		• Flaking food (fish) • Mixing ingredients together • Using a lemon squeezer

© The Food Teacher

Dietary Adaptations

Dairy free – soya yoghurt/mayonnaise

Mackerel Pâté
Serves 4

Equipment

Teaspoon
Tablespoon
Mixing spoon
Fork
Mixing bowl
Colander/sieve
Lemon juicer
Bowl for serving
Kitchen scissors

Ingredients

1 mackerel fillet (tin)
½ lemon or lime
12 fresh chives
2 tbsp. sour cream

Method

1. Squeeze the lemon/lime to remove the juice.
2. Flake the mackerel using a fork into the mixing bowl (**check for bones**).
3. Cut the chives using the scissors.
4. Mix the chives, lemon/lime juice and cream with the mackerel.
5. Mix thoroughly.
6. Spoon into your serving bowl.

(For serving – you could include rice crackers, oat cakes, carrot, cucumber, celery sticks)

Nutrition know how

Mackerel is an oily fish, which is high in omega-3 fatty acids. These are important for our brain to work and grow as these fats provide us with lots of energy. Omega-3 fatty acids may help our brain with learning and memory.

© The Food Teacher

Three Bean Salad
Serves 4-8

Learning Objectives

- Create a simple bean salad following a recipe
- Understand why legumes can benefit our health

Learning Outcomes

- Use of measuring spoons and whisk to create a dressing
- Prepared dish
- Can explain what legumes are and why they benefit our health

Aim

Children to create a simple bean salad

Assessment

- Skills
- Some awareness of the nutritional value of legumes

Skills Checklist

Knife Skills	Weighing and Measuring	Baking	Other
	• Using measuring spoons		• Washing and draining through a sieve/colander • Whisking (dressing) • Mixing ingredients together

© The Food Teacher

Three Bean Salad
Serves 4-8

Equipment

Teaspoon
Tablespoon
Mixing spoon
Whisk
Mixing bowl
Colander/sieve
Bowl for serving

Ingredients

1 tin (400g) cannelini beans
1 tin (400g) red kidney beans
1 tin (400g) black beans

For the dressing:
1 tsp. mustard
2 tbsp. balsamic vinegar
6 tbsp. olive oil

Method

1. Put the mustard, vinegar and olive oil into the mixing bowl and whisk together.
2. Open the tins of beans and pour into the colander/sieve (over the sink).
3. Rinse and drain the beans.
4. Pour the beans into the mixing bowl with the dressing.
5. Mix thoroughly.
6. Spoon into your serving bowl.

Nutrition know how

Kidney, black and cannellini beans are all known as legumes and grow from plants. They are a good source of iron, which is important for our red blood cells that carry oxygen around our bodies. This helps us to grow and gives us lots of energy.

© The Food Teacher

Veggie Kebabs
Serves 4

Learning Objectives

- Create a colourful vegetable snack
- Cut cucumber using the claw knife technique
- Understand why tomatoes benefit our health

Learning Outcomes

- Use a knife and cut cucumber using the claw knife technique
- Prepared dish
- Can explain why tomatoes are a healthy choice

Aim

Children to create a vegetable snack

Assessment

- Skills
- Some awareness of the nutritional value of tomatoes

Skills Checklist

Knife Skills	Weighing and Measuring	Baking	Other
• Claw knife technique	• Counting out ingredients		• Washing and draining through a sieve/colander

© The Food Teacher

Dietary Adaptations
Dairy free – dairy free hard cheese, cubed

NO KITCHEN COOKERY

Veggie Kebabs
Serves 4

Equipment

4 kebab sticks
Small knife for chopping
Chopping board
Plate for serving
Colander/sieve

Ingredients

Mozzarella pearls
8 cherry tomatoes
¼ cucumber
8 pitted olives/black grapes
Fresh basil leaves
Iceberg lettuce –for displaying the kebabs (optional)

Method

1. Wash your cucumber and tomatoes in the colander/sieve.
2. Chop your cucumber into slices.
3. Thread your ingredients onto the kebab sticks, alternating colours.
4. Put the pointed end into the lettuce at the end for display.

Nutrition know how

Tomatoes are actually a fruit. They are rich in vitamin C and a plant chemical called lycopene, which gives them their bright red colour. Lycopene has been known to protect the eyes, skin and support your body to fight germs and infections.

© The Food Teacher

Jewelled Rice/Pasta Salad
Serves 4-8

Learning Objectives

- Create a colourful salad following a recipe
- Cut herbs and vegetables using scissors
- Understand why a rainbow of colours can help to keep us healthy

Aim

Children to create a colourful salad

Assessment

- Skills
- Some awareness of the nutritional value of eating a rainbow

Learning Outcomes

- Use of scissors to cut
- Prepared dish
- Can explain what rainbow vegetables provide for our bodies

Skills Checklist

Knife Skills	Weighing and Measuring	Baking	Other
• Cutting using scissors	• Using measuring spoons • Using scales to check quantities		• Washing and draining through a sieve/colander • Mixing ingredients together (dressing)

© The Food Teacher

Jewelled Rice/Pasta Salad
Serves 4-8

Equipment

Teaspoon
Tablespoon
Mixing spoon
Kitchen scissors
Mixing bowl
Bowl for serving
Colander/sieve
Chopping board
Weighing scales

Ingredients

150g cold cooked rice/pasta
½ green pepper
½ orange pepper
4 dried apricots
100g tinned red kidney beans
Small bunch of fresh coriander
2 tbsp. olive oil

Method

1. Put the rice/pasta into the mixing bowl.
2. Use the scissors to cut the peppers and apricots into small pieces.
3. Add to the rice.
4. Open the tins of beans and pour into the colander/sieve (over the sink).
5. Rinse and drain the beans and add to the rice.
6. Cut up the coriander with the scissors and sprinkle into the bowl.
7. Pour the olive oil over the rice and mix thoroughly together.

Nutrition know how

If you eat a rainbow of colours from fruit and vegetables every day you will be eating a whole range of plant chemicals which provide many benefits to the body. These chemicals aren't essential like vitamins and minerals but they can help to keep our bodies working properly. Benefits include keeping our eyes and skin healthy and supporting us to fight germs and infections.

© The Food Teacher

Finger Sandwiches
Serves 4-8

Learning Objectives

- Prepare and create lunch/snack
- Spread and cut
- Understand why protein is important at every meal

Learning Outcomes

- Use of knives
- Prepared dish
- Can explain why protein is important at each meal

Aim

Children to make lunch/snack

Assessment

- Skills
- Some awareness of the importance of protein

Skills Checklist

Knife Skills	Weighing and Measuring	Baking	Other
• Bridge knife technique			• Spreading using a table knife (butter) • Cutting using cutters (shaped sandwiches)

Dietary Adaptations

Dairy free – dairy free spread

Vegetarian – choose meat free options

Finger Sandwiches
Serves 4-8

Equipment

Knife for spreading
Small knife for chopping
Chopping board
Biscuit cutters
Plate for serving

Ingredients

8 slices of bread
Butter/dairy-free spread
Sandwich fillings (cream cheese, sliced cheese, ham, hummus, tuna, cucumber, smoked salmon, lettuce)
Decoration – chives, cress

Method

1. Spread some butter onto one slice of bread.
2. Choose your filling and spread/layer over the butter.
3. Add the other slice on top and use a knife/cutters to cut into fingers, triangles, squares or shapes.
4. Decorate with paper flags, chives or cress.

Nutrition know how

Foods like meat, fish, cheese and hummus are rich in protein, which is needed for us to grow healthy and strong. It also helps to keep our concentration and energy levels even throughout the day so we need to think about eating protein with every meal.

© The Food Teacher

Fruit Kebabs
Serves 4

Learning Objectives

- Create a colourful fruit snack
- Cut strawberries using the bridge knife technique
- Understand that berries are a healthy choice

Learning Outcomes

- Use a knife and cut strawberries using the bridge knife technique
- Prepared dish
- Can explain why berries are a healthy choice

Aim

Children to create a fruit snack

Assessment

- Skills
- Some awareness of the nutritional value of berries

Skills Checklist

Knife Skills	Weighing and Measuring	Baking	Other
• Bridge knife technique	• Counting out ingredients		• Washing and draining through a sieve/colander

© The Food Teacher

Dietary Adaptations

If allergic to strawberries – choose different coloured grapes instead

Fruit Kebabs
Serves 4

Equipment

4 kebab sticks
Small knife for chopping
Chopping board
Plate for serving
Colander/sieve

Ingredients

Raspberries
Strawberries
Grapes
Blueberries

Method

1 Wash your berries and grapes in the colander/sieve.
2 Cut your strawberries in half.
3 Thread your ingredients onto the kebab sticks, alternating colours.

Nutrition know how

Berries contain lots of antioxidants, which are like 'superheroes' in your body helping to keep you fit and healthy. They tend to be found in lots of brightly coloured foods and help your digestion and keep your eyes and brain healthy.

© The Food Teacher

Avocado Orange Chocolate Mousse
Serves 4

Learning Objectives

- Create a dessert following a recipe
- Cut an avocado and mash until smooth
- Understand that avocados contain healthy fats

Learning Outcomes

- Use of measuring spoons, knife and masher
- Prepared dish
- Can explain why avocados are a healthy choice

Aim

Children to create a dessert

Assessment

- Skills
- Some awareness of the nutritional value of avocados

Skills Checklist

Knife Skills	Weighing and Measuring	Baking	Other
• Bridge knife technique	• Using measuring spoons		• Mashing • Mixing ingredients together • Using a lemon squeezer • Garnishing

© The Food Teacher

Avocado Orange Chocolate Mousse
Serves 4

Equipment

Fork
Small knife for chopping
Chopping board
Mixing bowl
Tablespoon
Lemon juicer
Grater
Bowls/ramekins for serving

Ingredients

2 ripe avocados
2 tbsp. cacao/cocoa
2 tbsp. honey/maple syrup
1 orange
Zest/Dark chocolate chunks for decoration (optional)

Method

1 Cut the avocado in half, squeeze slightly to remove the stone.
2 Squeeze all the flesh out of the skin into the mixing bowl.
3 Mash the avocado until smooth.
4 Squeeze the juice of the orange and add to the avocado.
5 Mix in the cocoa and honey and stir well.
6 Spoon into bowls and decorate with the zest/chocolate chunks.

Nutrition know how

Avocados are known as the fruit with the highest fat content. They contain monosaturated oils, which are really helpful to our bodies. These oils help to keep our blood pressure at healthy levels and keep all our joints healthy and supple.

Pineapple Smoothie
Serves 4

Learning Objectives

- Create a smoothie following a recipe
- Measure using a jug and scales
- Understand why pineapples can help our bodies

Learning Outcomes

- Use of measuring spoons, jug and lemon squeezer
- Prepared smoothie
- Can explain what pineapples contain for health

Aim

Children to create a smoothie

Assessment

- Skills
- Some awareness of the nutritional benefits of pineapples

Skills Checklist

Knife Skills	Weighing and Measuring	Baking	Other
• Bridge knife technique	• Using measuring spoons • Using balance scales • Using jug to measure		• Mashing • Mixing ingredients together • Using a lemon squeezer

© The Food Teacher

Dietary Adaptations

Dairy free – soya yoghurt/mayonnaise

Pineapple Smoothie
Serves 4

Equipment

Fork
Small knife for chopping
Chopping board
Bowl for mixing
Jug
Lemon juicer
Glasses/cups for serving
Teaspoon

Ingredients

2 small bananas
1 lime
1 tsp. runny honey
150g natural Greek yoghurt
½ pint (300ml) pineapple juice

Method

1. Peel the bananas and put them into the mixing bowl.
2. Use the fork to mash them until smooth and pour into the jug.
3. Cut the lime in half, squeeze out the juice and add the juice to the jug.
4. Put in the honey and mix well.
5. Add the yoghurt and pineapple juice and use the fork to whisk until frothy.
6. Pour into glasses/cups to serve.

Nutrition know how

Pineapples contain vitamin C and an enzyme called bromelain, which helps our digestion and to repair the body if we get injured. It also helps us to fight off germs and infections especially sore throats.

© The Food Teacher

Raspberry Punch
Serves 4

Learning Objectives

- Create a fruit drink following a recipe
- Cut oranges using a combination of bridge and claw technique
- Understand that berries are low in sugar and a healthy choice

Learning Outcomes

- Use a knife and cut using a combination of the claw and bridge technique
- Prepared smoothie
- Can explain why berries are a healthy choice

Aim

Children to create a fruit drink

Assessment

- Skills
- Some awareness of the nutritional value of berries

Skills Checklist

Knife Skills	Weighing and Measuring	Baking	Other
• Bridge knife technique	• Use a jug to measure		• Washing and draining through a sieve/colander • Mashing • Mixing ingredients together • Using a lemon squeezer

© The Food Teacher

Raspberry Punch
Serves 4

Equipment

Small knife for chopping
Potato masher
Chopping board
Lemon juicer
Colander/sieve
Mixing bowl
Glasses/cups for serving

Ingredients

4 oranges
1 small punnet of raspberries
330ml still/sparkling water

Method

1 Cut the oranges in half and juice them.
2 Pour the juice into the 4 glasses/cups.
3 Wash the raspberries in the colander/sieve and put them in the mixing bowl.
4 Mash the raspberries until them become a pulp.
5 Spoon the pulp into the 4 glasses/cups.
6 Slowly top up with the water.

Nutrition know how

Berries contain lots of antioxidants, which are like 'superheroes' in your body helping to keep you fit and healthy. They tend to be found in lots of brightly coloured foods and help your digestion and keep your eyes and brain healthy.

© The Food Teacher

Key Stage 2
Recipes

Guacamole
Serves 4

Learning Objectives

- Create a dip following a recipe
- Cut vegetables using a combination of bridge and claw technique
- Understand that avocados contain beneficial fats and are a healthy choice

Learning Outcomes

- Use a knife and cut a combination of the claw and bridge technique
- Prepared dip
- Can explain why avocados are a healthy choice

Aim

Children to create a dip for a snack or meal accompaniment

Assessment

- Skills
- Some awareness of the nutritional value of avocados

Skills Checklist

Knife Skills	Weighing and Measuring	Baking	Other
• Simple combination of bridge and claw technique • Fine chopping of herbs	• Using measuring spoons		• Mashing • Mixing ingredients together • Using a lemon squeezer • Crushing garlic

© The Food Teacher

Guacamole
Serves 4

Equipment

Fork
Small knife for chopping
Garlic press
Chopping board
Bowl for mixing
Jug
Lemon juicer
Bowl for serving
Teaspoon

Ingredients

2 ripe avocados
2 cloves of garlic
Lime
1 red onion
¼ red chili
1 large vine tomato
2 tbsp. fresh/frozen coriander
Black pepper

Method

1. Cut the avocado in half, squeeze slightly to remove the stone and squeeze all the flesh out of the skin into the mixing bowl.
2. Mash the avocado with a fork.
3. Squeeze the lime and add the juice to the avocado and mix well.
4. Finely chop the onion and add to bowl.
5. Finely chop the chilli and add to bowl.
6. Chop the tomato into small chunks and add to bowl.
7. Peel the garlic and crush in your crusher. Add to bowl.
8. Finely chop your coriander and add to bowl.
9. Stir the ingredients together and spoon into a serving bowl to serve.

Nutrition know how

Avocados are rich in vitamins and minerals and contain twice as much potassium as a banana. This is great for keeping blood pressure even. Avocados are also full of beneficial monounsaturated fats, great for growing brains.

© The Food Teacher

Coleslaw
Serves 6

Learning Objectives
- Create coleslaw following a recipe
- Grate harder foods
- Understand why cabbages are healthy

Learning Outcomes
- Use a grater to grate harder foods
- Prepared dip
- Can explain why cabbages are a healthy choice

Aim
Children to create a meal accompaniment

Assessment
- Skills
- Some awareness of the nutritional value of cabbages

Skills Checklist

Knife Skills	Weighing and Measuring	Baking	Other
- Simple combination of bridge and claw technique - Grating hard foods	- Using measuring spoons		- Washing and draining through a sieve/colander - Mixing/beating ingredients together (dressing)

© The Food Teacher

Dietary Adaptations
Dairy free – soya yoghurt/mayonnaise

Coleslaw
Serves 6

Equipment

Fork
Small knife for chopping
Grater
Jug
Chopping board
Bowl for mixing
Bowl for serving
Teaspoon
Tablespoon

Ingredients

3 tbsp. Greek natural yoghurt
½ tsp. Dijon mustard
1 tbsp. cider vinegar
½ small white cabbage
2 carrots
½ onion

Method

1 In the jug combine the yoghurt, mustard and vinegar stirring well.
2 Wash the carrots in running water.
3 Use the grater to grate the carrots and cabbage and put into your bowl.
4 Finely chop your onion and add to the bowl.
5 Pour the dressing onto the vegetables and mix well.
6 Spoon into your serving bowl to serve.

Nutrition know how

Cabbages are bitter foods, which help our bodies, digest our food. They contain vitamin C, K and antioxidants that help to protect our skin and provide our liver with beneficial nutrients.

© The Food Teacher

Couscous Salad
Serves 4

Learning Objectives

- Create couscous following a recipe
- Cut vegetables using a combination of bridge and claw technique
- Understand that sweet peppers are a healthy choice

Learning Outcomes

- Use a knife and cut a combination of the claw and bridge technique
- Can explain why sweet peppers are a healthy choice

Aim

Children to create a lunch

Assessment

- Skills
- Some awareness of the nutritional value of sweet peppers

Skills Checklist

Knife Skills	Weighing and Measuring	Baking	Other
• Simple combination of bridge and claw technique	• Using measuring spoons • Use a jug to measure • Use balance scales		• Washing and draining through a sieve/colander • Mixing ingredients together • Crumbling (feta) • Garnishing

© The Food Teacher

Dietary Adaptations

Dairy free – omit the feta and replace with dairy-free cheese

Couscous Salad
Serves 4

Equipment

Kettle (hot water)
Fork
Small knife for chopping
Jug
Small plate
Chopping board
Bowl for mixing
Bowl for serving
Teaspoon
Tablespoon
Weighing scales

Ingredients

100g couscous
200ml hot water
¼ tsp. Bouillon powder (veg stock)
2 spring onions
1 red pepper
½ cucumber
50g feta cheese
2 tbsp. pesto
2 tbsp. pine nuts/mixed seeds

Method

1. Pour the water into the jug and stir in the bouillon.
2. Add the couscous to the hot water, stir and cover with the plate.
3. Finely slice the onion, pepper and add to mixing bowl.
4. Dice the cucumber and add to the bowl.
5. Check the couscous has absorbed all the water and use a fork to mix up.
6. Pour the couscous into the bowl, add the pesto and mix well.
7. Pour into the serving bowl and crumble over the feta.
8. Sprinkle the pine nuts on top and serve.

Nutrition know how

Sweet peppers are a member of the nightshade family, which includes tomatoes and potatoes. They contain vitamin C and antioxidants, which help to protect our eyes and our hearts as we get older.

© The Food Teacher

Chunky Hummus
Serves 4

Learning Objectives

- Create hummus following a recipe
- Crush garlic and use a masher
- Understand what legumes are

Learning Outcomes

- Use a garlic press and masher
- Prepared dip
- Can explain what legumes are

Aim

Children to create a snack

Assessment

- Skills
- Some awareness of the nutritional value of legumes

Skills Checklist

Knife Skills	Weighing and Measuring	Baking	Other
	• Using measuring spoons		• Washing and draining through a sieve/colander • Mashing • Using a lemon squeezer • Crushing garlic • Mixing ingredients together

© The Food Teacher

Chunky Hummus
Serves 4

Equipment

Fork
Potato masher
Small knife for chopping
Chopping board
Garlic press
Colander/sieve
Jug
Lemon juicer
Bowl for mixing
Bowl for serving
Teaspoon
Tablespoon

Ingredients

1 tin (400g) chickpeas
2 tsp. lemon juice
1 garlic clove
1 tsp. ground cumin
3 tbsp. tahini
Water
2 tbsp. olive oil
1 tsp. paprika

Method

1. Empty the chickpeas into the sieve/colander and rinse under running water.
2. Use the fork/masher to crush the chickpeas into a mash.
3. Peel the garlic and crush in the press. Add to bowl.
4. Squeeze the lemon and add the juice.
5. Add the tahini, olive oil and cumin.
6. Mix well and slowly add tbsp. of water to create a creamy chunky texture.
7. Spoon into the serving bowl and sprinkle with the paprika to serve.

(For serving – you could include rice crackers, oat cakes, carrot, cucumber, celery sticks)

Nutrition know how

Chickpeas are legumes and grow from plants. They are a good source of iron, which is important for our red blood cells that carry oxygen around our bodies. This helps us to grow and give us lots of energy.

Egg Mayonnaise Spiders
Serves 4

Learning Objectives

- Create a snack following a recipe
- Can decorate prepared snack (spiders legs)
- Understand why eggs are a healthy choice

Learning Outcomes

- Use bridge knife technique
- Prepared snack
- Can explain why eggs are a healthy choice

Aim

Children to create a fun snack

Assessment

- Skills
- Some awareness of the nutritional value of eggs

Skills Checklist

Knife Skills	Weighing and Measuring	Baking	Other
• Bridge knife technique	• Using measuring spoons		• Shelling a hard boiled egg • Mixing ingredients together • Garnishing and decorating

Dietary Adaptations

Dairy free – soya yoghurt/mayonnaise

© The Food Teacher

Egg Mayonnaise Spiders
Serves 4

Equipment

Fork
Small knife for chopping
Chopping board
Bowl for mixing
Plate for serving
Tablespoon
Teaspoon

Ingredients

4 hard-boiled eggs
2 tbsp. natural Greek yogurt
12 pitted black olives

Method

1 Peel the hard boiled eggs.
2 Cut in half and scoop the yellow yolk into the bowl.
3 Use the fork to mash the egg yellows and add the yoghurt stirring well.
4 Cut the olives in half keeping 8 for the spider body.
5 Cut the other halves into 4 spider legs each.
6 Spoon the egg mayonnaise mixture into the egg whites.
7 Then decorate with the olives to create your spiders.
8 Place onto your serving plate to serve.

Nutrition know how

Eggs are a good source of good quality protein. They also contain vitamin D, which is important for our bone and teeth growth. Egg yolks contain antioxidants which help to protect our eyes and they are also a great source of choline, B vitamins and fats that provide fuel to our brains helping us to learn and remember.

© The Food Teacher

Pitta Pockets
Serves 4

Learning Objectives

- Create lunch/snack using your own recipe
- Understand why protein is important for our bodies

Learning Outcomes

- Use a toaster
- Prepared lunch/snack
- Can explain why protein is important for our bodies

Aim

Children to create a snack/lunch

Assessment

- Skills
- Plan for own recipe
- Some awareness of the nutritional value of protein

Skills Checklist

Knife Skills	Weighing and Measuring	Baking	Other
• Bridge knife technique • Claw knife technique • Grating hard and soft foods			• Washing and draining through a sieve/colander • Using a toaster

© The Food Teacher

Dietary Adaptations

Gluten free pitta bread (do not use toaster as cross contamination risk)

Pitta Pockets
Serves 4

Equipment

Knife
Small knife for chopping
Chopping board
Bowl for mixing
Plate for serving
Tablespoon
Teaspoon
Toaster

Ingredients

4 wholemeal pitta breads
Fillings (cream cheese, cheese, ham, hummus, tuna, smoked salmon, cucumber, grated carrot, tomato, lettuce)

Method

1 Cut the pitta bread into 2 pockets and lightly toast until opened.
2 Fill the pitta pocket with a filling of your choice.
3 Place on your serving plate to serve.

Nutrition know how

Foods like meat, fish, cheese and hummus are rich in protein, which is needed for us to grow healthy and strong. It also helps to keep our concentration and energy levels even throughout the day so we need to think about eating protein with every meal.

© The Food Teacher

Greek Salad
Serves 6

Learning Objectives

- Create lunch following a recipe
- Can use the appropriate knife techniques for different tasks
- Understand the health benefits of onions

Learning Outcomes

- Use appropriate knife techniques for different tasks
- Prepared lunch
- Can explain the health benefits of onions

Aim

Children to create a lunch

Assessment

- Skills
- Some awareness of the health benefits of onions

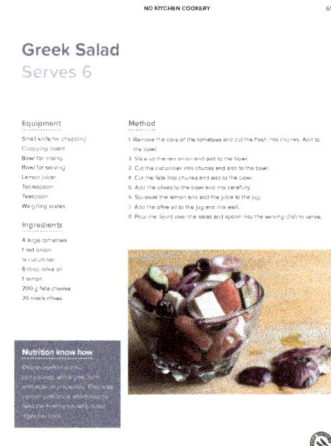

Skills Checklist

Knife Skills	Weighing and Measuring	Baking	Other
• Bridge knife technique • Claw knife technique • Simple combination of techniques	• Using measuring spoons • Using balance scales • Using digital or spring balance scales		• Washing and draining through a sieve/colander • Mixing ingredients together • Using a lemon squeezer

© The Food Teacher

Dietary Adaptations

Dairy free – omit feta for chicken/tuna/ dairy free cheese

Greek Salad
Serves 6

Equipment

Small knife for chopping
Chopping board
Bowl for mixing
Bowl for serving
Lemon juicer
Tablespoon
Teaspoon
Weighing scales

Ingredients

4 large tomatoes
1 red onion
¼ cucumber
6 tbsp. olive oil
1 lemon
200 g feta cheese
20 black olives

Method

1. Remove the core of the tomatoes and cut the flesh into chunks. Add to the bowl.
2. Slice up the red onion and add to the bowl.
3. Cut the cucumber into chunks and add to the bowl.
4. Cut the feta into chunks and add to the bowl.
5. Add the olives to the bowl and mix carefully.
6. Squeeze the lemon and add the juice to the jug.
7. Add the olive oil to the jug and mix well.
8. Pour the liquid over the salad and spoon into the serving dish to serve.

Nutrition know how

Onions contain sulphur compounds, which give them antibacterial properties. They also contain prebiotics, which help to feed the healthy bacteria in our digestive tract.

Sour Cream and Chive Dip
Serves 4

Learning Objectives

- Create dip following a recipe
- Can snip herbs in a jug
- Understand that herbs can benefit our cooking and health

Learning Outcomes

- Use appropriate knife techniques for different tasks
- Prepared lunch
- Can explain that herbs can benefit our cooking and health

Aim

Children to create a snack

Assessment

- Skills
- Some awareness of the health benefits of herbs

Skills Checklist

Knife Skills	Weighing and Measuring	Baking	Other
• Snipping herbs in a jug using scissors • Claw knife technique	• Using measuring spoons • Using jug to measure		• Washing and draining through a sieve/colander • Mixing ingredients together • Using a lemon squeezer

© The Food Teacher

Dietary Adaptations

Dairy free sour cream (may need to order)

Sour Cream and Chive Dip
Serves 4

Equipment

Kitchen scissors
Cup
Jug
Bowl for mixing
Bowl for serving
Tablespoon
Teaspoon
Chopping board
Small knife for cutting
Weighing scale

Ingredients

25g fresh chives
300 ml sour cream
1 tsp. lemon juice
Carrot and cucumber for dipping

Method

1. Put the chives in a cup and use the kitchen scissors to chop into tiny pieces.
2. Save 1 tbsp. of chives in the cup and add the rest to the mixing bowl.
3. Squeeze the lemon and add the juice to the bowl.
4. Pour the sour cream into the bowl and mix well.
5. Spoon into the serving bowl and top with the saved chives.
6. Cut up some carrot and cucumber sticks for serving.

(For serving – you could include rice crackers, oat cakes, carrot, cucumber, celery sticks)

Nutrition know how

We call herbs, such as chives and rosemary culinary herbs, which provide flavour in our food and provide healthful properties. They can have antibacterial effects and help our digestion.

Paprika Dip
Serves 4

Learning Objectives

- Create dip following a recipe
- Can use the claw knife technique
- Understand that yoghurt contains 'healthy' bacteria

Learning Outcomes

- Use appropriate knife techniques for different tasks
- Prepared lunch
- Can explain why probiotics are beneficial for our health

Aim

Children to create a snack

Assessment

- Skills
- Some awareness of the health benefits of 'healthy' bacteria

Skills Checklist

Knife Skills	Weighing and Measuring	Baking	Other
• Claw knife technique	• Using measuring spoons • Using balance scales		• Washing and draining through a sieve/colander • Mixing ingredients together • Crushing garlic

© The Food Teacher

Dietary Adaptations

Dairy free soya yoghurt and dairy free cream cheese (may need to order)

Paprika Dip
Serves 4

Equipment

Knife
Small knife for chopping
Chopping board
Garlic press
Bowl for mixing
Bowl for serving
Tablespoon
Teaspoon
Weighing scales

Ingredients

300g cream cheese
1 tsp. tomato purée
2 tbsp. natural Greek yoghurt
2 spring onions
1 garlic clove
2 tsps. paprika

Method

1. Put the cream cheese in a bowl and add the tomato purée and 1 tbsp. of the yoghurt. Mix well then add the rest of the yoghurt. Mix again.
2. Slice the spring onions into small pieces and add to the bowl.
3. Crush the garlic and add the paprika. Stir well.
4. Spoon into the serving bowl to serve.

(For serving – you could include rice crackers, oat cakes, carrot, cucumber, celery sticks)

Nutrition know how

Natural yoghurt contains 'healthy' bacteria, which live in our digestive tract and help with our absorption of food. These bacteria also help to strengthen our immune system helping us to fight germs.

© The Food Teacher

Spiral Sandwiches/Wraps
Serves 4

Learning Objectives

- Create lunch/snack using your own recipe
- Can roll bread/wraps to create a spiral
- Understand why adding vegetables to sandwiches is healthy

Learning Outcomes

- Use a rolling pin and knife to create spirals
- Prepared lunch/snack
- Can explain why adding vegetables to sandwiches is healthy

Aim

Children to create a lunch/snack

Assessment

- Skills
- Plan for own recipe
- Some awareness of the nutritional value of vegetables

Skills Checklist

Knife Skills	Weighing and Measuring	Baking	Other
• Bridge knife technique • Claw knife technique			• Washing and draining through a sieve/colander • Spreading ingredients • Using a rolling pin

© The Food Teacher

Dietary Adaptations

Offer appropriate choices for dietary requirements

Spiral Sandwiches/Wraps
Serves 4

Equipment

Knife
Rolling pin
Small knife for chopping
Chopping board
Plate for serving
Tablespoon
Teaspoon

Ingredients

8 slices of bread/wraps
Butter/dairy-free spread
Sandwich fillings (cream cheese, sliced cheese, ham, hummus, tuna, smoked salmon, cucumber, grated carrot, lettuce)

Method

1. If using bread, roll a rolling pin over each slice a few times. Use a sharp knife to cut off the crusts.
2. Spread each piece with butter and add a thick layer of filling.
3. Roll up each slice/wrap into a sausage shape and cut into smaller pieces.
4. Put onto a plate to serve.

Nutrition know how

Vegetables mixed with protein help to give our bodies a range of nutrients that keep our digestion healthy, blood sugars balanced and energy levels high.

Layered Rainbow Salad
Serves 4

Learning Objectives

- Create a layered rainbow salad using your own recipe
- Can use the appropriate knife techniques for different tasks
- Understand why eating a rainbow of colours is healthy

Learning Outcomes

- Use the appropriate knife techniques for different tasks
- Prepared lunch/dinner
- Can explain why eating a rainbow of colours is healthy

Aim

Children to create a lunch/dinner

Assessment

- Skills
- Plan for own recipe
- Some awareness of the nutritional value of eating a rainbow of colours every day

Skills Checklist

Knife Skills	Weighing and Measuring	Baking	Other
- Bridge knife technique - Claw knife technique	- Using measuring spoons		- Washing and draining through a sieve/colander - Shelling a hard boiled egg - Garnishing and decorating

Dietary Adaptations

Offer appropriate choices for dietary requirements

Layered Rainbow Salad
Serves 4

Equipment

Small knife for chopping
Chopping board
Glass bowl for serving
Tablespoon
Sieve/colander

Ingredients

Choose different ingredients for layering thinking about colours.

Choose from red (peppers, tomato, radishes, red onion), orange (peppers, carrots), yellow (pepper, hard boiled eggs, sweetcorn), green (peas, cucumber, lettuce, pepper, avocado) and black (olives).

Method

1 Plan the different layers of your salad.
2 Chop and prepare each vegetable layer, then add to your serving bowl.
3 Once all your layers are added you can serve.

Nutrition know how

A rainbow of vegetables every day is beneficial because we increase our intake of naturally occurring chemicals (phytonutrients), which give the foods their colours. Different colours provide different benefits. Find out when salad foods are in season.

© The Food Teacher

Make Your Own Muesli
Serves 4

Learning Objectives

- Create a breakfast muesli using your own recipe
- Can use the appropriate knife techniques for different fruits
- Understand that dried fruit is high in sugar so use minimally to provide some natural sweetness

Learning Outcomes

- Use of the appropriate knife techniques for different fruits
- Prepared breakfast muesli
- Can explain why dried fruit is high in sugar

Aim

Children to create a breakfast muesli

Assessment

- Skills
- Plan for own recipe
- Some awareness of the sugar content in dried fruit

Skills Checklist

Knife Skills	Weighing and Measuring	Baking	Other
• Bridge knife technique • Claw knife technique	• Using measuring spoons		• Washing and draining through a sieve/colander • Mixing ingredients together

© The Food Teacher

Dietary Adaptations

Offer appropriate choices for dietary requirements

Make Your Own Muesli
Serves 4

Equipment

Small knife for chopping
Chopping board
Bowl for mixing
Bowl for serving
Dessert spoon
Container for storing
Tablespoon
Teaspoon

Ingredients

Choose different ingredients to create a unique recipe.

Choose from rolled oats, quinoa flakes, puffed brown rice, puffed millet, dried apple, soft dates, soft apricots, dried mango, dried banana, dried berries, coconut chips, sunflower seeds, linseeds, pumpkin seeds, poppy seeds.

Fresh milk and fruit for serving.

Method

1. Plan the different ingredients for your muesli.
2. Chop and prepare the different ingredients and combine together in a bowl.
3. Spoon into your container to keep fresh.
4. Try a portion with milk and add some fresh fruit (berries, bananas).

Nutrition know how

Dried fruit is high in sugar because the drying process removes the water content and the sugar becomes more concentrated. Eat dried fruit in moderation to provide natural sweetness.

Avocado and Lime Mousse
Serves 4

Learning Objectives

- Create a dessert following a recipe
- Can use a grater to remove zest
- Understand that honey is a natural sweetener

Learning Outcomes

- Use a grater to remove zest
- Prepared dessert
- Can explain that honey is a natural sweetener

Aim

Children to create a dessert

Assessment

- Skills
- Some awareness that honey is a natural sweetener and therefore a healthier choice

Skills Checklist

Knife Skills	Weighing and Measuring	Baking	Other
- Bridge knife technique - Grating soft foods - Finer grating	- Using measuring spoons		- Mashing - Mixing ingredients together - Using a lemon squeezer

© The Food Teacher

Avocado and Lime Mousse
Serves 4

Equipment

Small knife for chopping
Fork
Chopping board
Bowl for mixing
Bowl for serving
Tablespoon
Grater
Lemon juicer
Teaspoon

Ingredients

2 ripe avocados
3 limes
1 tsp. vanilla extract
2 tbsp. honey/maple syrup

Method

1. Cut the avocado in half, squeeze slightly to remove the stone and squeeze all the flesh out of the skin into the mixing bowl.
2. Use the fork to mash until smooth.
3. Grate the limes removing the zest.
4. Cut the limes in half and squeeze out the juice.
5. Add the zest, juice, vanilla extract and honey to the bowl and mix well.
6. Pour into a bowl to serve.

Nutrition know how

Honey is a natural sweetener which contains dextrose and fructose sugars. As it is natural it also contains vitamins and minerals, which provide other benefits to our bodies.

© The Food Teacher

NO KITCHEN COOKERY

Green Smoothie
Serves 4

Learning Objectives

- Create a healthy green smoothie using your own recipe
- Can use the appropriate knife techniques for different tasks
- Understand that green leaves are highly nutritious

Learning Outcomes

- Use the appropriate knife techniques for different tasks
- Prepared smoothie
- Can explain that green leaves are highly nutritious

Aim

Children to create a 'healthy' green smoothie

Assessment

- Skills
- Plan for own recipe
- Some awareness that green leaves are highly nutritious

Skills Checklist

Knife Skills	Weighing and Measuring	Baking	Other
• Simple combination of bridge and claw technique	• Using measuring spoons • Using a jug to measure liquids		• Washing and draining through a sieve/colander • Using a blender

© The Food Teacher

Dietary Adaptations
Offer appropriate choices for dietary requirements

Green Smoothie
Serves 4

Equipment

Small knife for chopping
Chopping board
Jug/measuring cup
Blender

Ingredients

2 cups spinach/kale
2 cups liquid – water/coconut water/coconut milk/almond milk
3 cups fruit (mixture) – banana/mango/berries/avocado/peach/grapes

Method

1. Wash your green leaves in the colander/sieve and drain.
2. Place into the blender with your chosen liquid.
3. Blend together.
4. Prepare and chop your chosen fruit and add to the green liquid.
5. Blend again until smooth.
6. Pour into glasses/cups to serve.

Nutrition know how

Spinach and kale both contain vitamin K, which helps to strengthen our bones. They also contain calcium and iron, which can be easily absorbed by the body from these foods.

Apricot Seed Bars
Serves 12

Learning Objectives

- Create a healthy snack following a recipe
- Using a blender
- Understand that apricots are highly nutritious

Learning Outcomes

- Using a blender (pulse ingredients)
- Prepared snack bars
- Can explain that apricots are highly nutritious

Aim

Children to create a 'healthy' snack

Assessment

- Skills
- Plan for own recipe
- Some awareness that apricots are highly nutritious

Skills Checklist

Knife Skills	Weighing and Measuring	Baking	Other
• Bridge knife technique • Grating soft foods	• Using measuring spoons • Using digital or spring balance scales		• Beating ingredients together • Using a blender • Lining a tin with parchment paper • Pressing mixture into a baking tin

© The Food Teacher

Dietary Adaptations

Dairy free – coconut oil

Apricot Seed Bars
Serves 12

Equipment

Small knife for chopping
Chopping board
Square baking tin
Parchment paper
Tablespoon
Teaspoon
Blender
Hob/microwave
Container for storage
Weighing scales

Ingredients

120g coconut oil/butter, room temperature
200g mixed seeds (sunflower, pumpkin)
60g jumbo oats
30g ground flaxseeds
250g soft, dried apricots, chopped
1 orange

> **Nutrition know how**
>
> Apricots are rich in fibre and vitamins A, C and E, ideal for digestive health, eyes and skin.

Method

1. Melt the coconut oil/butter if necessary, otherwise stir till soft.
2. Blend the oats and seeds to form a flour.
3. Grate the orange and add the zest to the bowl.
4. Add the other ingredients into the blender and pulse until mix resembles breadcrumbs.
5. Stir in the melted coconut oil/butter.
6. Press into a square tin lined with parchment paper.
7. Chill in the fridge for at least an hour.
8. Remove and cut into bars and store in the fridge.

Nutrition Know How

Macronutrients

Nutrient	Food Sources	Recipes	Function
Fats	Meat, fish, dairy foods, coconut oil, avocados, nuts and seeds, olive oil	KS1: 16, 18, 24, 28, 34, 40, 42 KS2: 48, 50, 56, 60, 64, 66, 68, 72, 80, 84	A good balance of polyunsaturated, monosaturated and saturated is needed for optimal health, brain and nerve function, energy and metabolism. Helps us to absorb fat soluble vitamins A, D E and K.
Protein	Meat, dairy, legumes (beans, chickpeas), wholegrains, nuts and seeds	KS1: 16, 18, 20, 24, 26, 28, 32, 34, 40, 42 KS2: 48, 50, 52, 56, 58, 64, 66, 68, 72, 74, 76, 80, 84	Needed for growth and repair of body tissues and for hormones and enzymes.
Carbohydrates	Wholegrains (rice, pasta, bread), oats, potatoes, legumes, cereal	KS1: 20, 26, 32, 34 KS2: 52, 60, 72, 76, 84	Good source of energy. Healthier choice is to choose complex carbohydrates rather then white, processed grains.
Fibre	Wholegrains, legumes, fruit and vegetables, nuts and seeds	KS1: 16, 20, 26, 28, 32, 34, 36, 40, 42, 44 KS2: 48, 50, 52, 56, 60, 64, 72, 74, 76, 80, 82, 84	Important for digestive health, lowers cholesterol and regulates appetite.

© The Food Teacher

Macronutrients — Vitamins

B Vitamins (Water soluble – so sources best steamed or raw)

Nutrient	Food Sources	Recipes	Function
Vitamin A (Fat soluble)	Liver, carrots, apricots, dark green leafy vegetables, fish	KS1: 16, 18, 24, 32, 34 KS2: 50, 52, 72, 74, 76, 82, 84	Antioxidant, which quenches damaging free radicals. Beneficial for sight, growth and repair, bones and teeth.
B1 – Thiamin B2 – Riboflavin B3 – Niacin B5 – Pantothenic Acid B6 – Pyridoxine B9 – Folic Acid	Yeast extract (Marmite), liver, fish (tuna), meat, nuts and seeds, wholegrains, avocado	KS1: 16, 18, 20, 24, 26, 34, 40 KS2: 48, 52, 60, 72, 76, 80, 84	Use fats and protein to release energy. Important for cell growth, nervous system, hormones and digestion.
Vitamin B12 – Cobalamin	Liver, shellfish, oily fish, eggs, meat, dairy	KS1: 16, 18, 24, 28, 34 KS2: 50, 58, 60, 64, 66, 68, 72	Used for cell formation including red blood cells, therefore important for healthy nervous system, blood cells, digestive system and skin. Deficiency linked to anaemia (low red blood cells, pale skin, low energy). Plants do not contain bioactive forms – imp. for vegans to supplement/ fortified foods, e.g. Marmite
Vitamin C	Rainbow of fruit and vegetables: dark green leafy vegetables, sweet peppers, berries	KS1: 16, 28, 32, 34, 36, 44 KS2: 50, 52, 60, 64, 72, 74, 82, 84	Antioxidant supporting healthy immune system, wound healing, bones, teeth and gums. Supports absorption of iron. High temperatures can reduce levels.
Vitamin D	Oily fish, seeds, dairy, mushrooms, fortified foods (cereals)	KS1: 16, 18, 24 KS2: 58, 64, 66, 76, 84	Needed for calcium absorption, therefore important for bones and teeth, healthy immunity, nervous system support and hormone balance.
Vitamin E	Nuts and seeds, oils (olive), wholegrains, avocados, tomatoes, broccoli	KS1: 16, 20, 26, 32, 34, 40 KS2: 48, 52, 56, 60, 68, 80, 84	Antioxidants supporting healthy immune system, skin, tissue healing, circulation, hormones, fertility and growth.
Vitamin K	Dark green leafy vegetables, turnip, oats, legumes	KS1: 20, 26, 32, 34 KS2: 56, 60, 72, 74, 76, 82, 84	Needed for energy, bone health, blood sugar balance, skin and immunity.

© The Food Teacher

Major Minerals

These minerals are required by the body in larger quantities.

Nutrient	Food Sources	Recipes	Function
Calcium	Seaweed, dairy, dark green leafy vegetables, legumes, broccoli, almonds	KS1: 16, 18, 20, 24, 26, 28, 32, 34, 42 KS2: 50, 56, 58, 60, 64, 66, 68, 72, 74, 82, 84	Most abundant mineral in body. For bones and teeth, hormones, nerves and muscles and blood pressure.
Phosphorus	Nuts and seeds, cheese, chicken, eggs, lentils	KS1: 28, 34 KS2: 58, 60, 64, 66, 72, 76	Needed to support healthy bones, and energy production.
Potassium Sodium Chloride	Nuts and seeds, spinach, mushrooms, broccoli, banana, red meat	KS1: 34 KS2: 60, 72, 76, 82, 84	All electrolytes – mineral salts that conduct electricity when dissolved in water. Regulate blood pressure, water balance, hormone, muscle and nerve health.
Sulphur	Eggs, legumes, wholegrains, garlic, onions, brussel sprouts, cabbage	KS1: 20, 26, 32, 34 KS2: 48, 50, 52, 56, 58, 60, 64, 72, 74, 76	Needed for protein structure such as joints, hair, nails and skin.
Magnesium	Kelp, seaweed, nuts and seeds, spinach, apricots, dates, avocado	KS1: 16, 32, 40 KS2: 48, 52, 64, 74, 76, 82, 84	Important for bone strength, nerve and muscle function. Also needed for tissue repair and energy production.

Trace Minerals

Nutrient	Food Sources	Recipes	Function
Chromium	Liver, beef, wholegrains, potatoes	KS1: 32, 34 KS2: 52, 60, 72, 76, 84	Supports blood sugar balance and cholesterol regulation.
Copper	Nuts, butter, legumes, seafood	KS1: 16, 20, 26, 34 KS2: 52, 56, 60, 72, 76, 84	Needed for iron absorption, red blood cells, skin, bones and nerves.

© The Food Teacher

Nutrient	Food Sources	Recipes	Function
Iodine	Seaweed, shellfish, dark green leafy vegetables	KS1: 16, 32, 34 KS2: 52, 60, 64, 72, 74, 82	For metabolism and optimal function of thyroid gland and production of hormones.
Iron	Clams, molasses, nuts and seeds, liver	KS1: 16, 32, 34 KS2: 52, 60, 64, 72, 74, 82, 84	Needed for red blood cell function, energy release and growth. Also important for healthy skin and nails. Vitamin C enhances absorption.
Manganese	Nuts, spinach, oats, avocado	KS1: 40 KS2: 48, 52, 74, 82, 84	Antioxidant important for bone formation and brain health.
Selenium	Oats, tuna, garlic, eggs	KS1: 18, 34 KS2: 48, 56, 58, 76, 84	Antioxidant that works with vitamin E. Important for reproduction, thyroid health and body repair.
Zinc	Oysters, ginger, red meat, nuts and seeds, legumes	KS1: 20, 26, 34 KS2: 52, 56, 60, 72, 76, 84	Antioxidant and immune system regulator. Important for wound healing, skin, hair and muscle health and growth.

Other Nutrients

Nutrient	Food Sources	Recipes	Function
Essential fatty Acids – Omega Oils	Oily fish, milk, oils (linseed, walnut, hempseed)	KS1: 16, 18, 24, 40 KS2: 48, 52, 56, 58, 64, 76, 80, 84	Important to regulate inflammation, growth, brain function, nervous system, eyes, skin, circulation, heart, hormone and joint health.
Phytonutrients – Plant chemicals – e.g. quercitin, rutin	Rainbow of fruit and vegetables	KS1: 16, 28, 32, 34, 36, 40, 42, 44 KS2: 48, 50, 52, 60, 64, 72, 74, 80, 82, 84	Antioxidants supporting healthy immunity, growth, repair, brain function, nervous system, circulation, eyes, skin, joints, metabolism and hormones.

© The Food Teacher

Glossary

Beat	To mix ingredients together using a fast, circular movement with a fork, spoon or whisk
Blend	To mix ingredients together gently using a fork or spoon
Breadcrumbs	Finely grated or ground mixture made from bread
Bridge Knife Cut	To make a bridge with the thumb and index finger and holding the knife under the bridge cut downwards
Claw Knife Cut	To shape your fingers into a claw, which rests on the food and as the food is sliced the claw slowly moves away from the knife
Chill	To cool down an ingredient or a dish by placing in the fridge
Chop	To cut into small pieces
Chunks	To cut into large pieces
Combine	To mix together
Core	The central part of the food, which contains the seeds
Crush	To squeeze something very hard to break it into smaller parts
Cut	To make something smaller using scissors or a knife
Decorate	To make something look more interesting before serving
Dice	To cut into small cubes
Drain	To remove the liquid
Equipment	The tools that are needed for a particular recipe
Flake	To break up an ingredient into smaller, thin pieces
Garnish	To decorate food before serving
Grate	To scrape food against the holes of a grater to make small pieces
Ingredients	The foods which are used in a recipe to create a dish
Juice	The liquid that can be squeezed out of fruit and vegetables
Julienne	To cut food into long, thin strips

© The Food Teacher

Line	Cover a baking tray/tin with paper or butter so food doesn't stick to it
Mash	To squash food with a fork, masher or spoon
Melt	To slowly heat a food to turn it into a liquid
Mix	To stir ingredients together with a fork or spoon
Peel	To remove the skin of a fruit or vegetable
Pour	To tip one food into a bowl or onto other foods
Press	To push or squeeze something firmly
Pulp	A soft, wet mixture made when food is mashed/pressed
Pulse	Short, fast blends or beating of a mixture
Recipe	The instructions for how to prepare a food/dish
Rinse	To use water to clean off a food
Roll	To make something smooth and flat using a rolling pin
Season	To improve the flavour of a food by adding herbs or spices
Serve	To prepare food or drinks ready to be eaten
Separate	To divide up ingredients, e.g. separate the egg yolk from the white
Scoop	To dig out a substance to put somewhere else
Slice	To cut off a thin, piece of food from a larger piece
Snip	To cut something with scissors
Spread	To use a knife to cover something with a softer food, e.g. to cover a piece of bread with butter
Sprinkle	To drop a few pieces of a food on the top of a dish
Squeeze	To press something firmly to remove the liquid
Stir	To mix ingredients together using a circular movement using a fork, spoon or whisk
Tear	To pull/break something apart using your fingers
Thread	To push foods onto a stick
Toast	To warm a food up by putting it near heat
Wash	To clean a food off in water
Whisk	To beat foods together to add air and make the food lighter
Zest	Skin of an orange, lemon or lime, which can be used to add flavour to food

How The Food Teacher Can Help You

As The Food Teacher, Katharine works with schools in various ways depending on staff and pupil needs, funding and priority. Many schools utilise grants such as Pupil Premium or the Sports and PE grant to fund work with The Food Teacher.

Katharine has extensive experience working with schools offering advisory support, developing curriculum content, schemes of work, assessment, policy development, mentoring staff and model and team teaching. Measuring the impact of her support is an inclusive aspect of her work.

She will also review or develop school menus working with caterers, help facilitate 'Pupil Voice' groups, plan themed school food and nutrition days or workshops for children and parents, set up school farmers markets and establish local community partnerships, e.g. with sports professionals, farmers and allotments.

The Food Teacher clinic can provide consultations and will work with individual children and their families through schools. These programmes can impact significantly on learning and pupil progress by improving pupil nutrition. They are bespoke to individual needs and may involve reducing obesity risk, improving concentration, attendance (boosting immunity), supporting reluctant eaters, focusing on behaviour and supporting children with special educational needs.

Please contact **The Food Teacher** to discuss your needs further.
Email: info@thefoodteacher.co.uk

www.thefoodteacher.co.uk

Lightning Source UK Ltd.
Milton Keynes UK
UKHW050201220319
339617UK00002B/34/P